Christmas
Theme

Colouring Book

De-ann Black

Published 2020

ISBN: 9798694927451

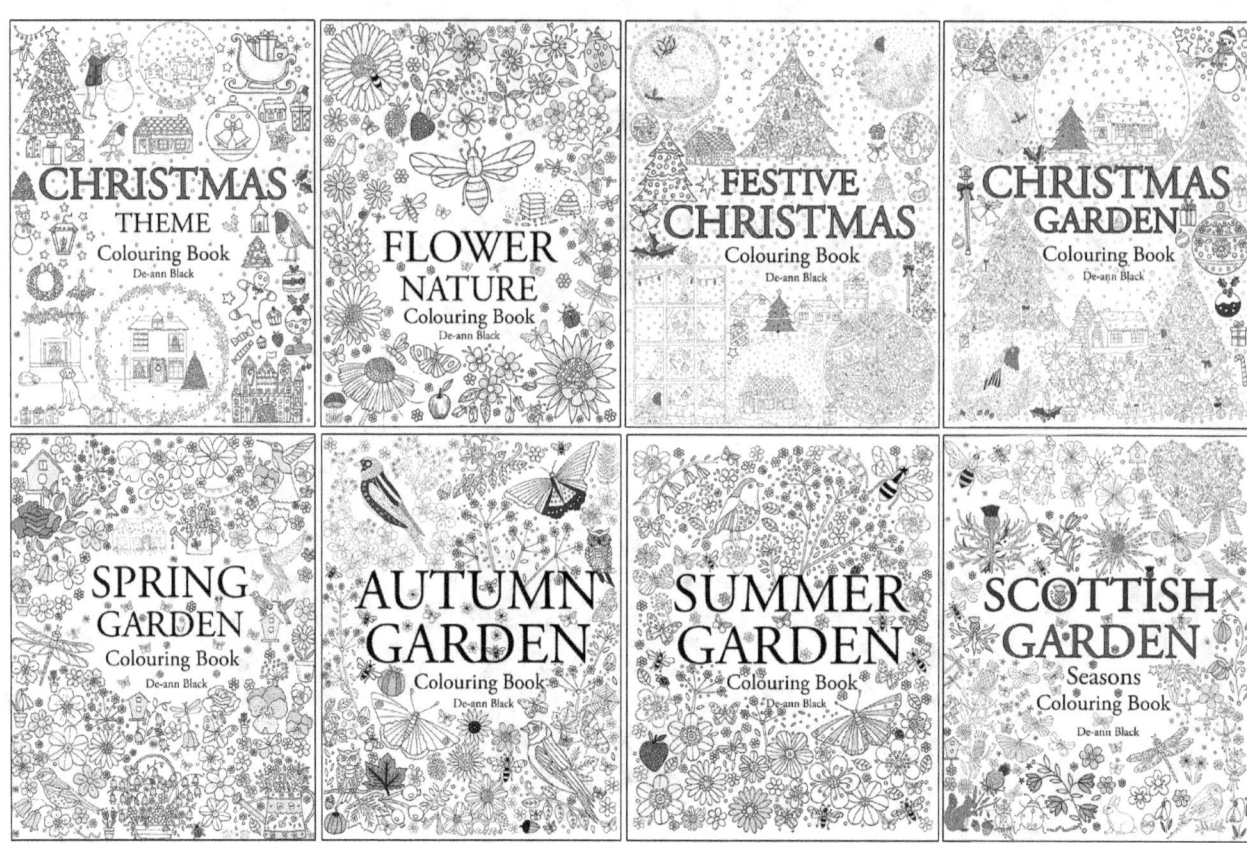

Colouring books by De-ann Black include: Sea Dream, Flower Bee, Bee Garden, Flower Hunter, Wild Garden, Faerie Garden Spring and Stargazer Space.

Romance:

The Sewing Bee
The Quilting Bee
Snow Bells Wedding
Snow Bells Christmas
Summer Sewing Bee
The Chocolatier's Cottage
Christmas Cake Chateau
The Beemaster's Cottage
The Sewing Bee By The Sea
The Flower Hunter's Cottage
The Christmas Knitting Bee
The Sewing Bee & Afternoon Tea
The Tea Shop
Shed In The City
The Bakery By The Seaside
Champagne Chic Lemonade Money
The Christmas Chocolatier
The Christmas Tea Shop & Bakery
Dublin Girl - Hot Summer In The City
Oops! I'm The Paparazzi
The Cure For Love

Embroidery books:

Floral Nature Embroidery Designs
Scottish Garden Embroidery Designs.

Crime/Thrillers:

Love Him Forever
Someone Worse
Electric Shadows
The Strife Of Riley
Shadows Of Murder

Children's books:

Faeriefied
Secondhand Spooks
Poison-Wynd
Science Fashion
School For Aliens
Wormhole Wynd

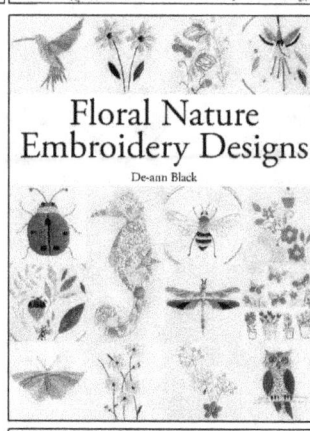

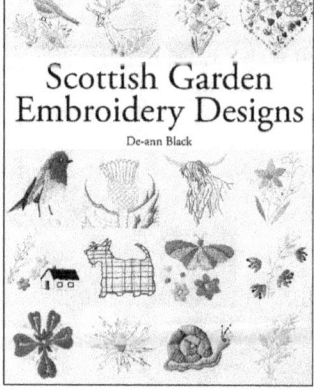

Further details about De-ann's books, art, illustrations and fabric designs are available from her website - www.De-annBlack.com

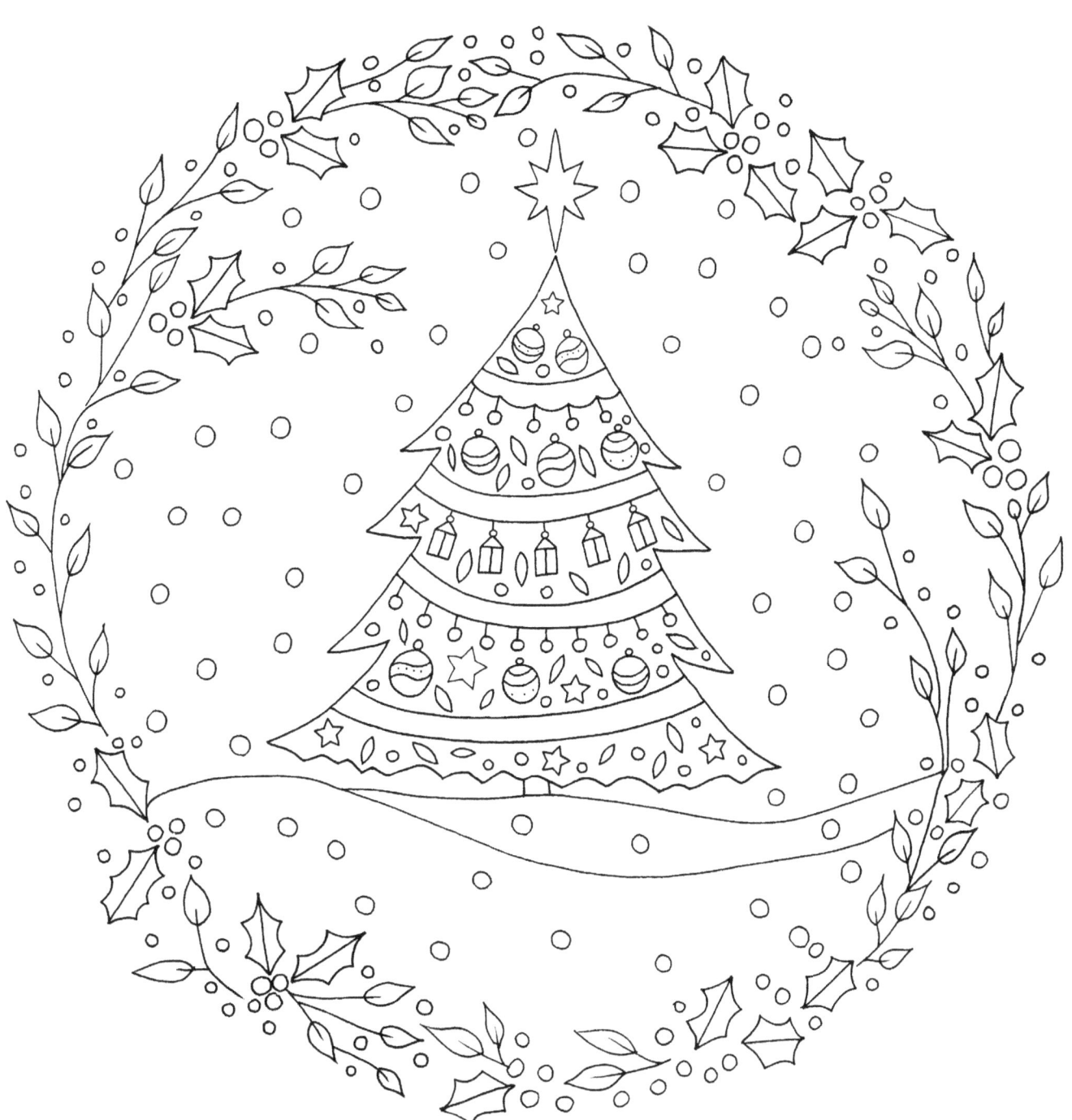

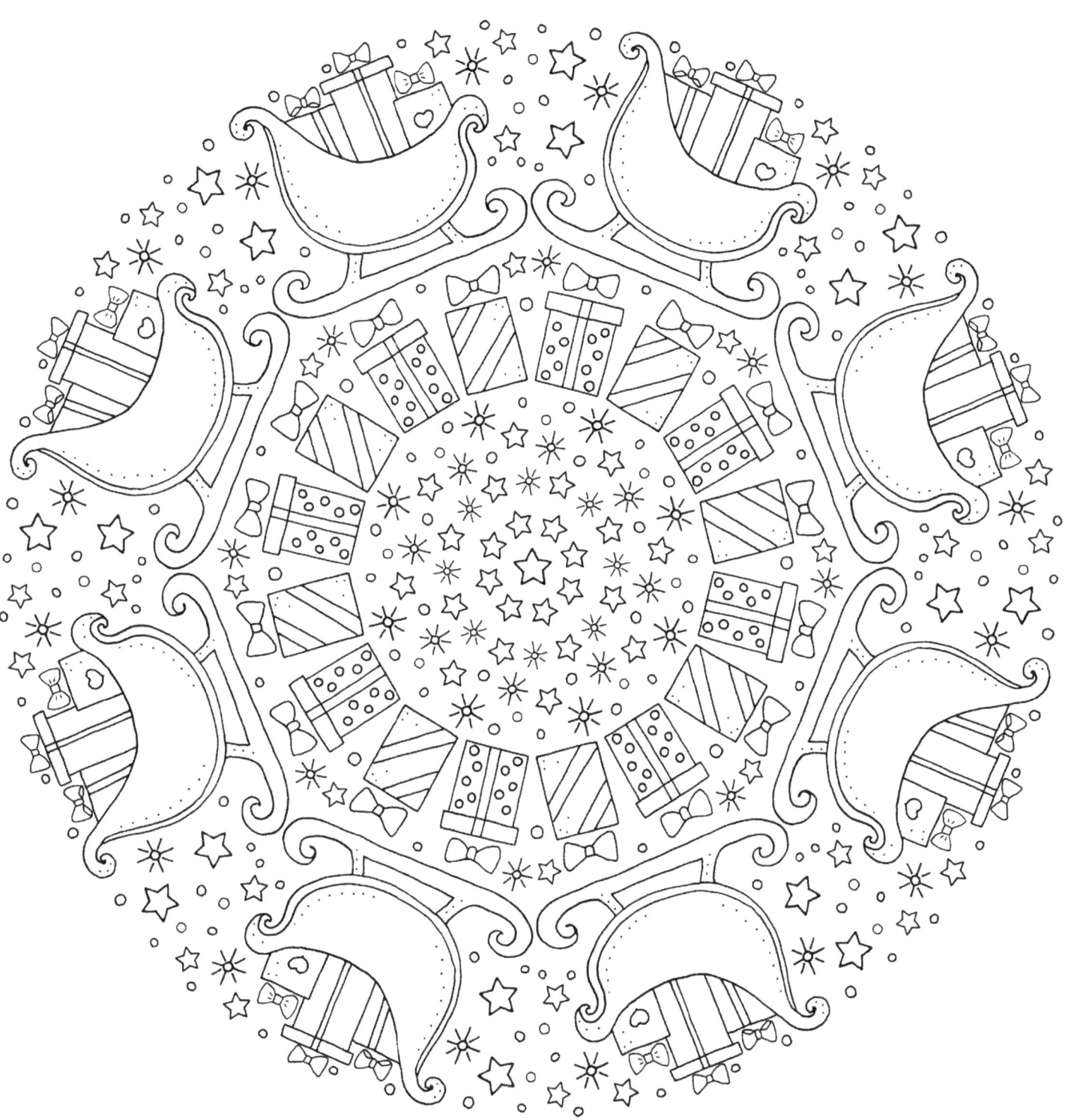

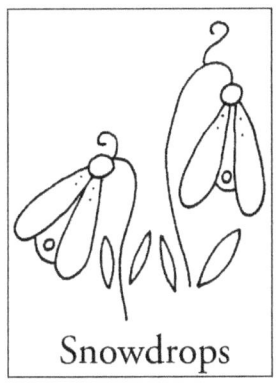

Snowdrops

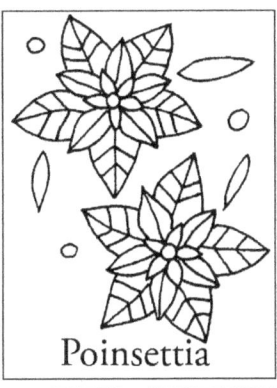

Poinsettia

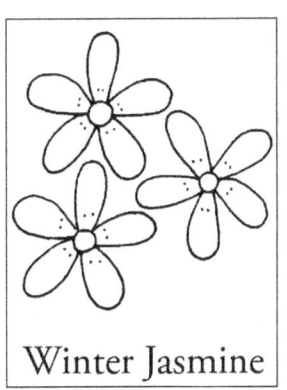

Winter Jasmine

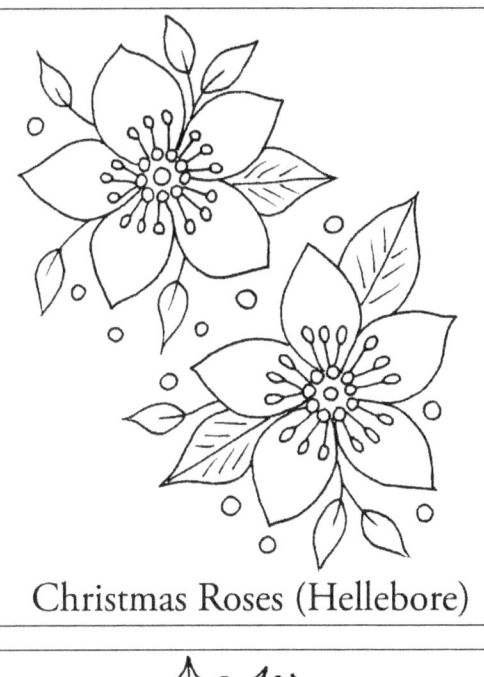

Christmas Roses (Hellebore)

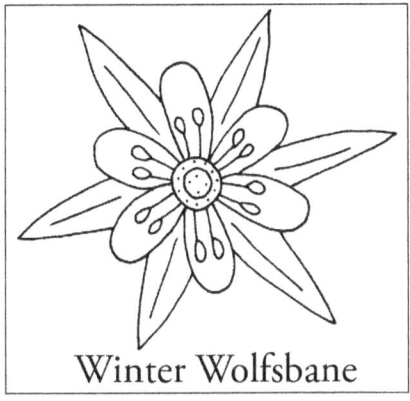

Winter Wolfsbane

Michaelmas Daisy

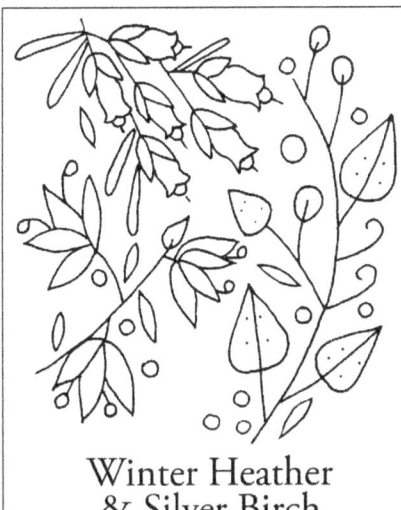

Winter Heather
& Silver Birch

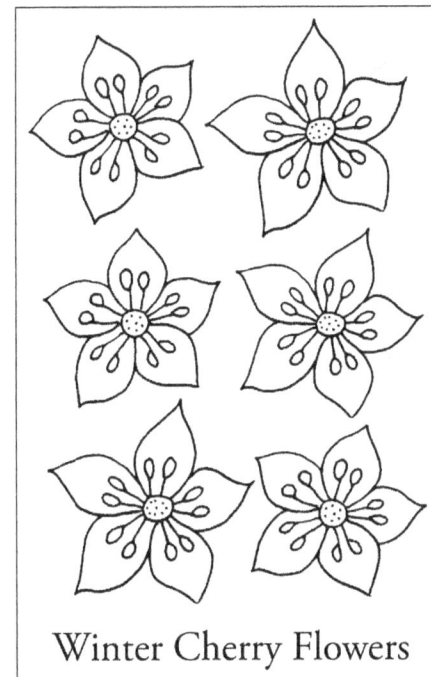
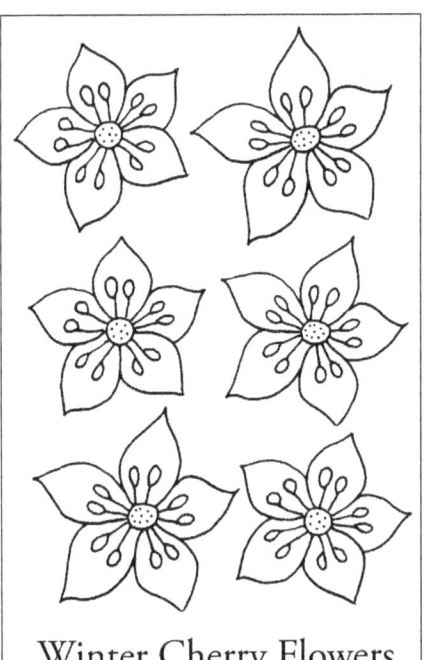

Winter Cherry Flowers

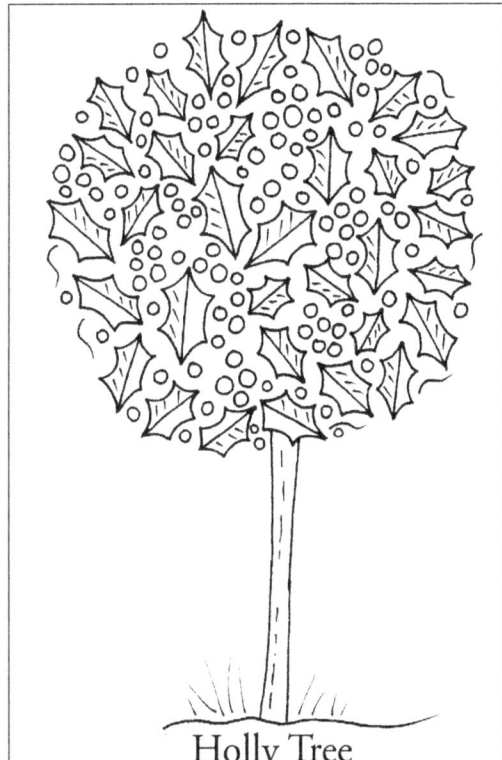

Holly Tree

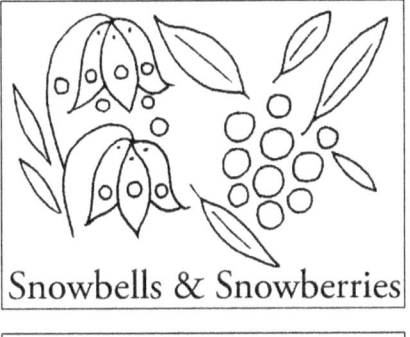

Snowbells & Snowberries

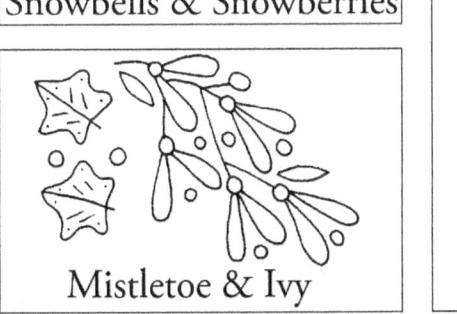

Mistletoe & Ivy

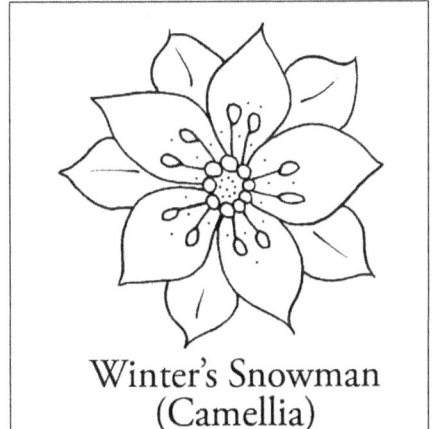

Winter's Snowman
(Camellia)

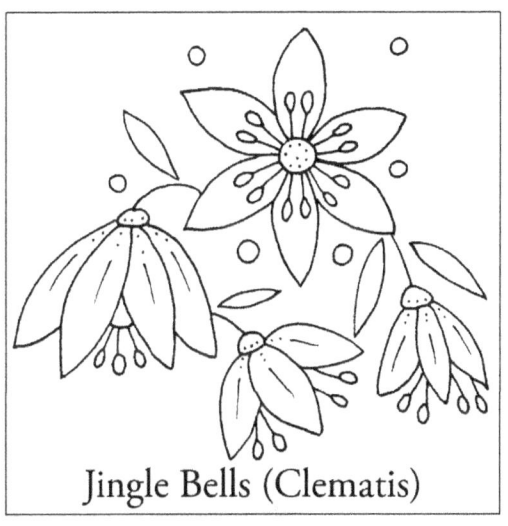

Jingle Bells (Clematis)

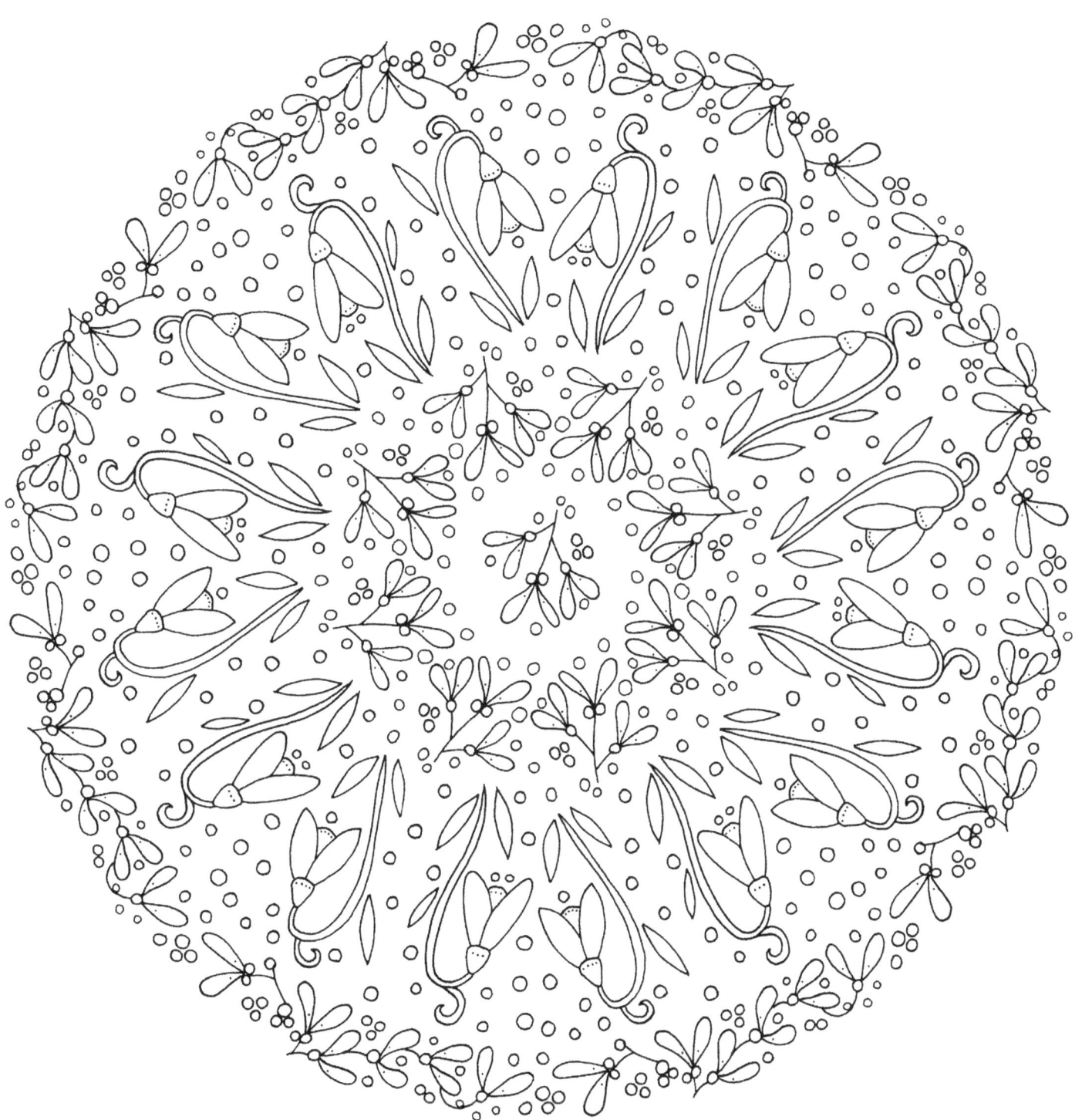

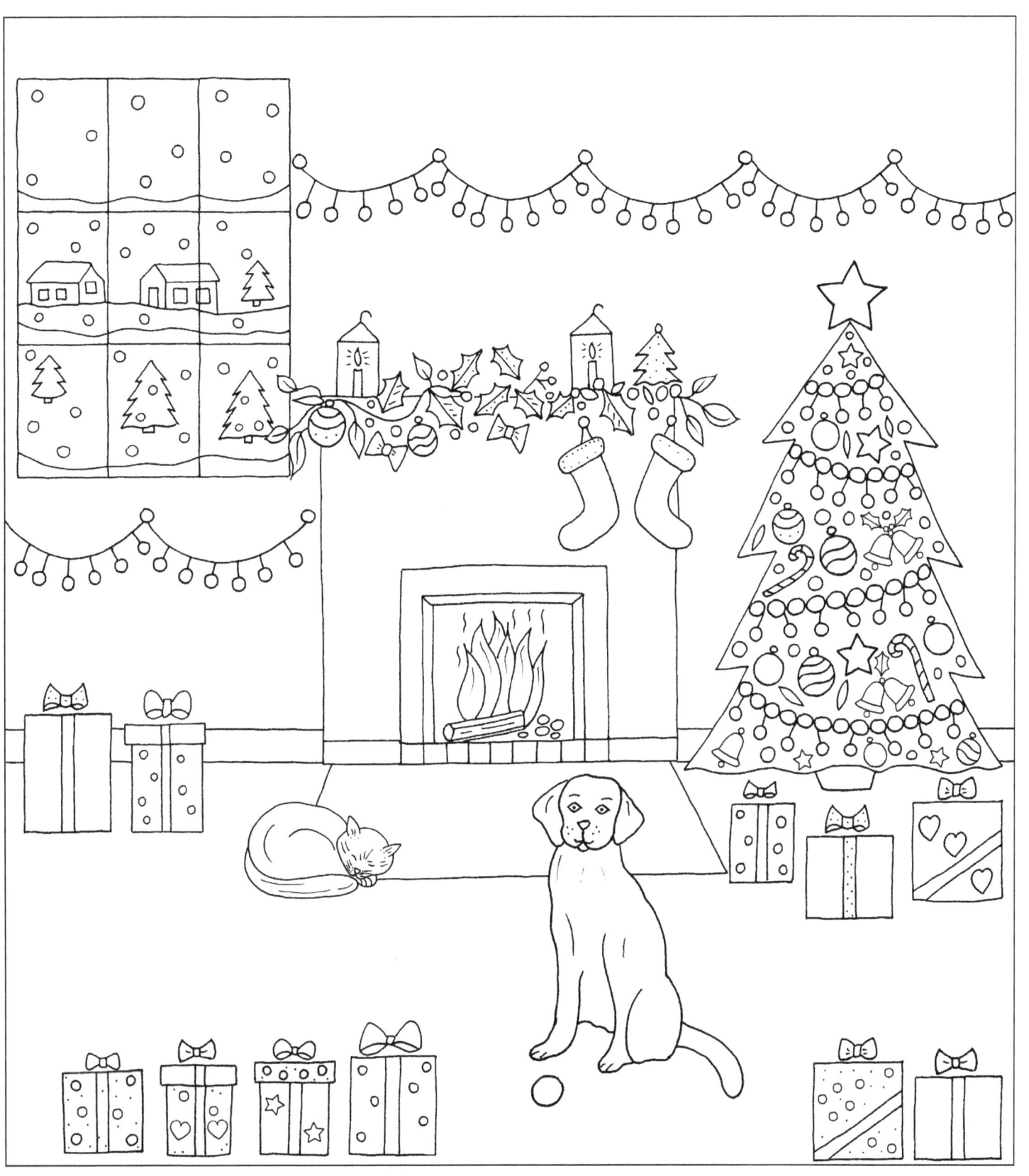

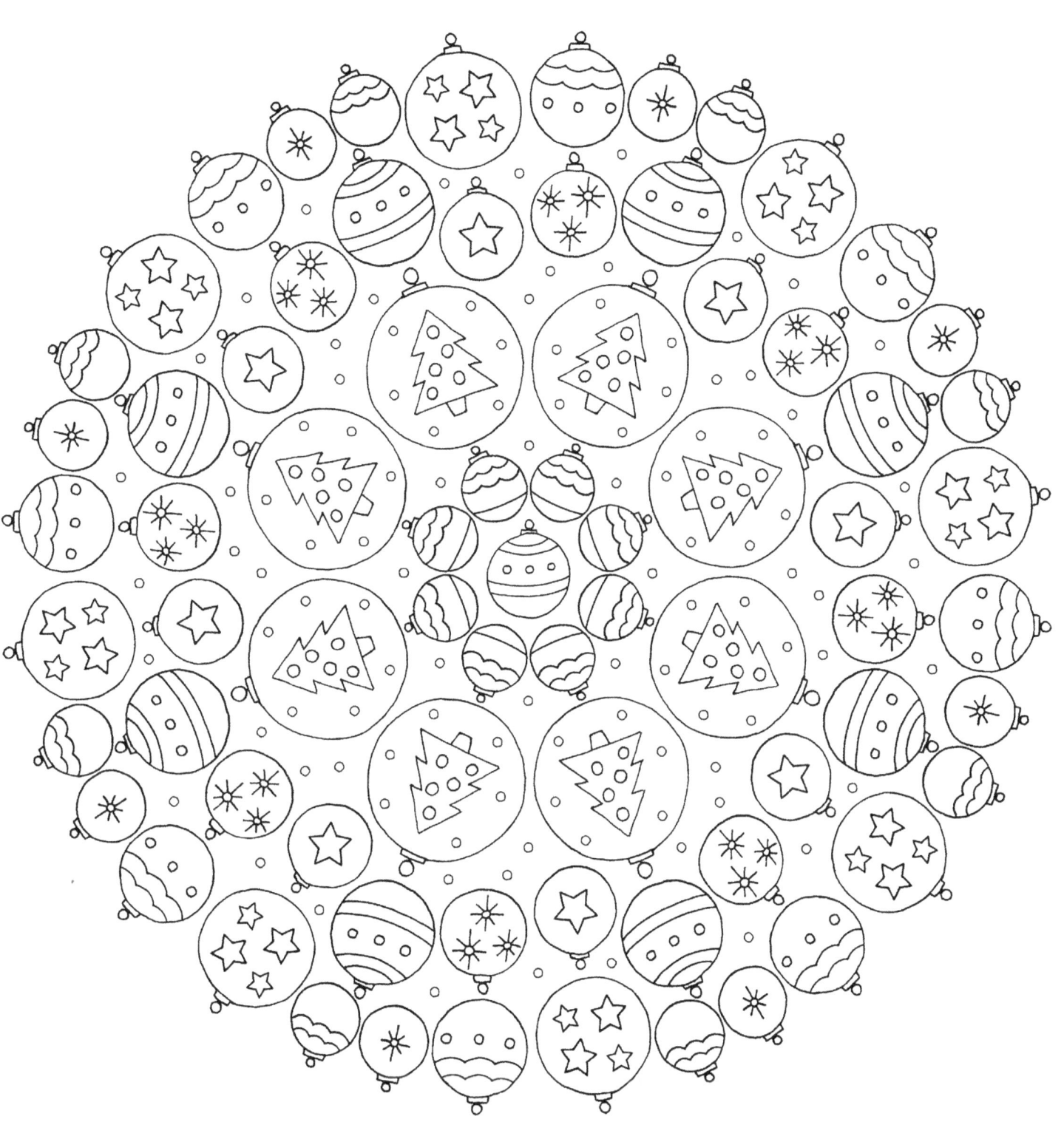

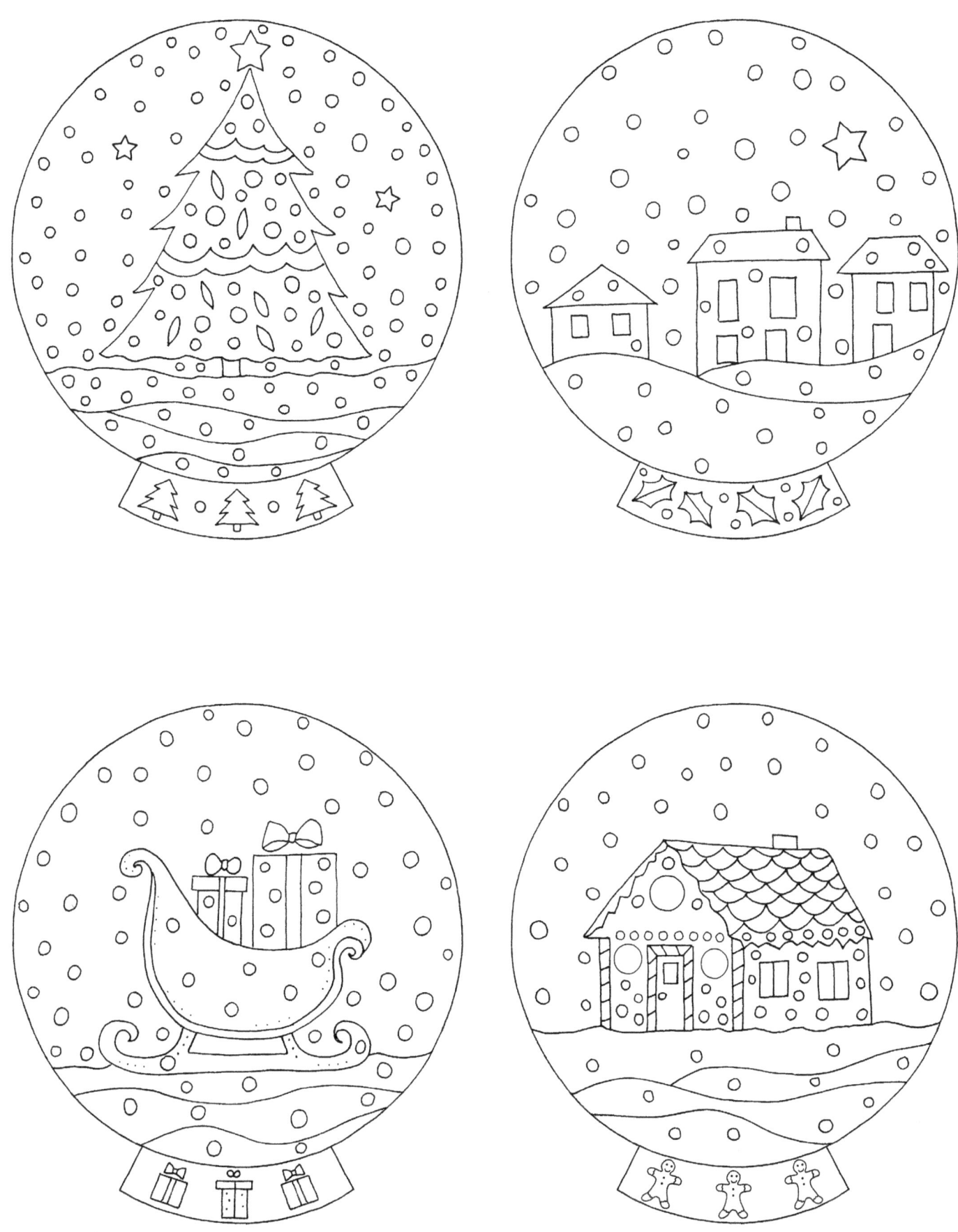

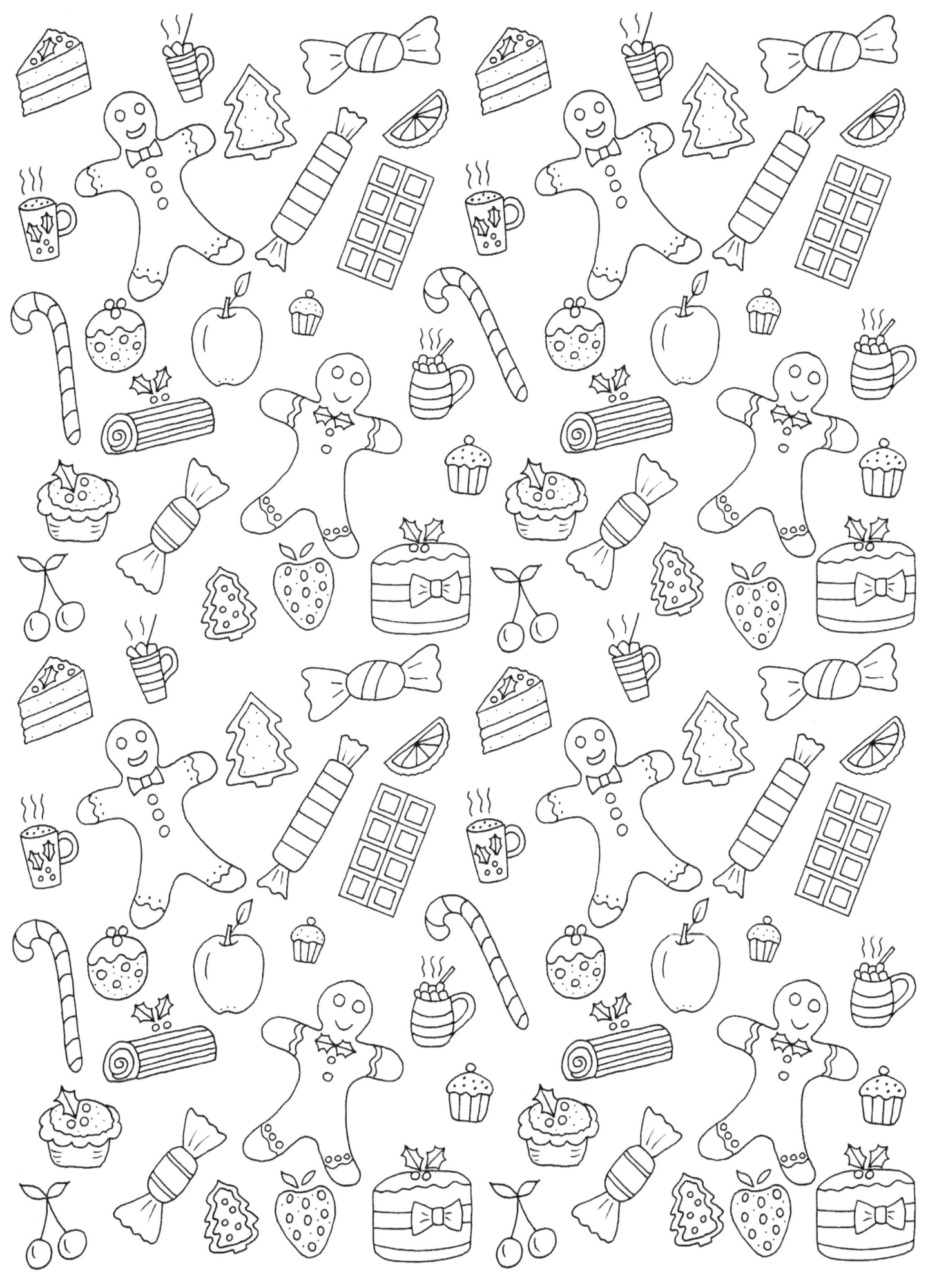

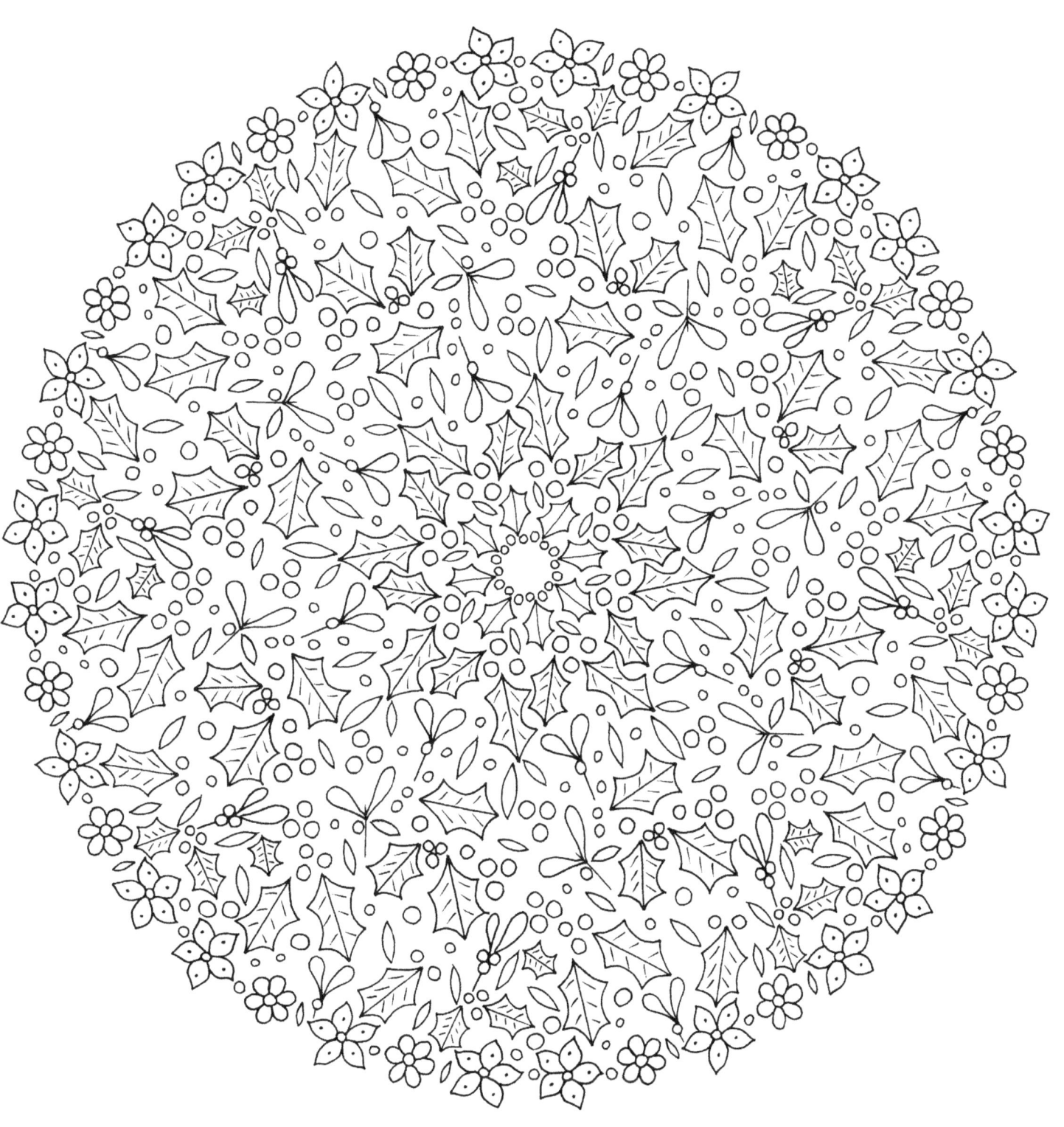

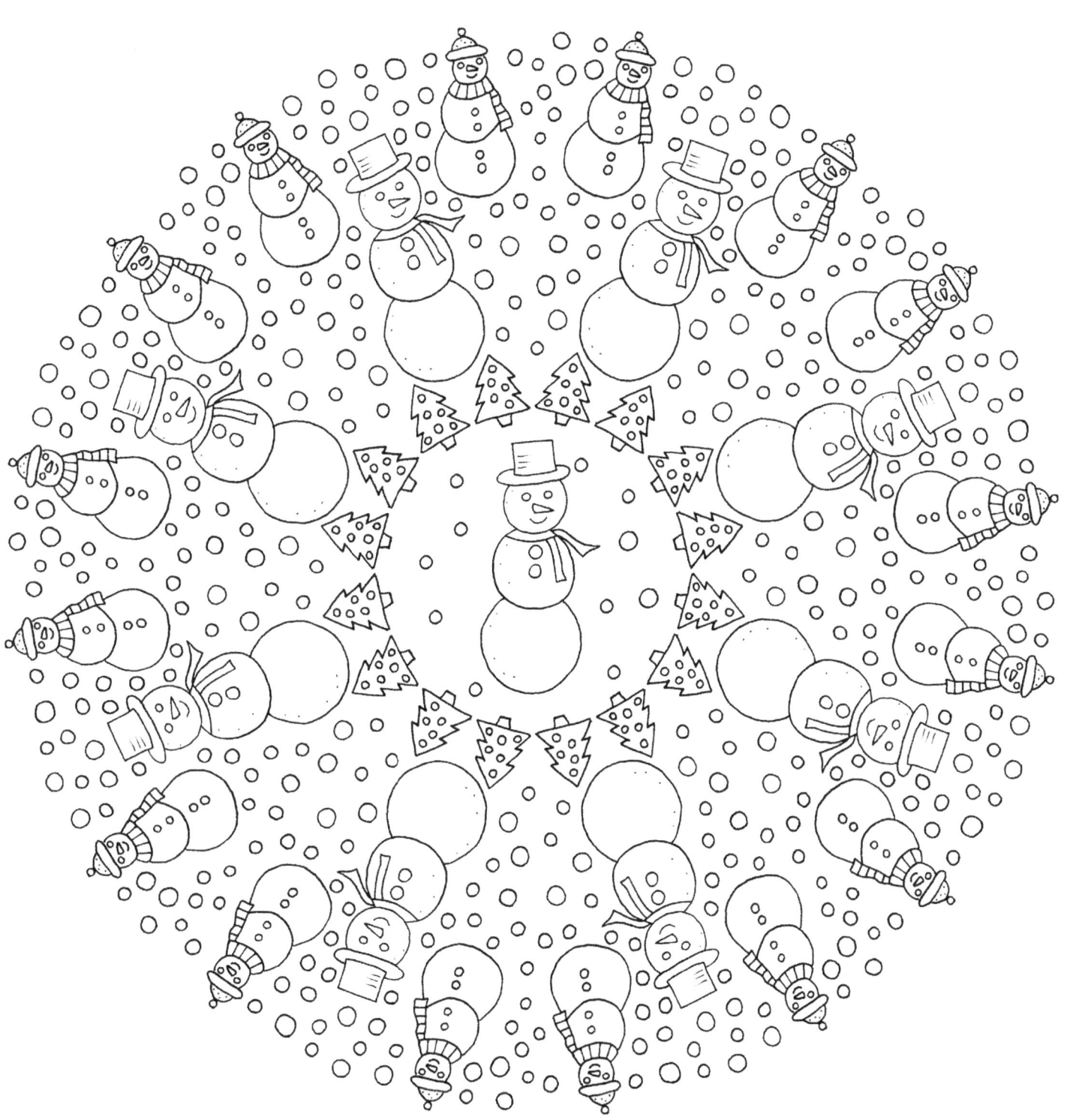

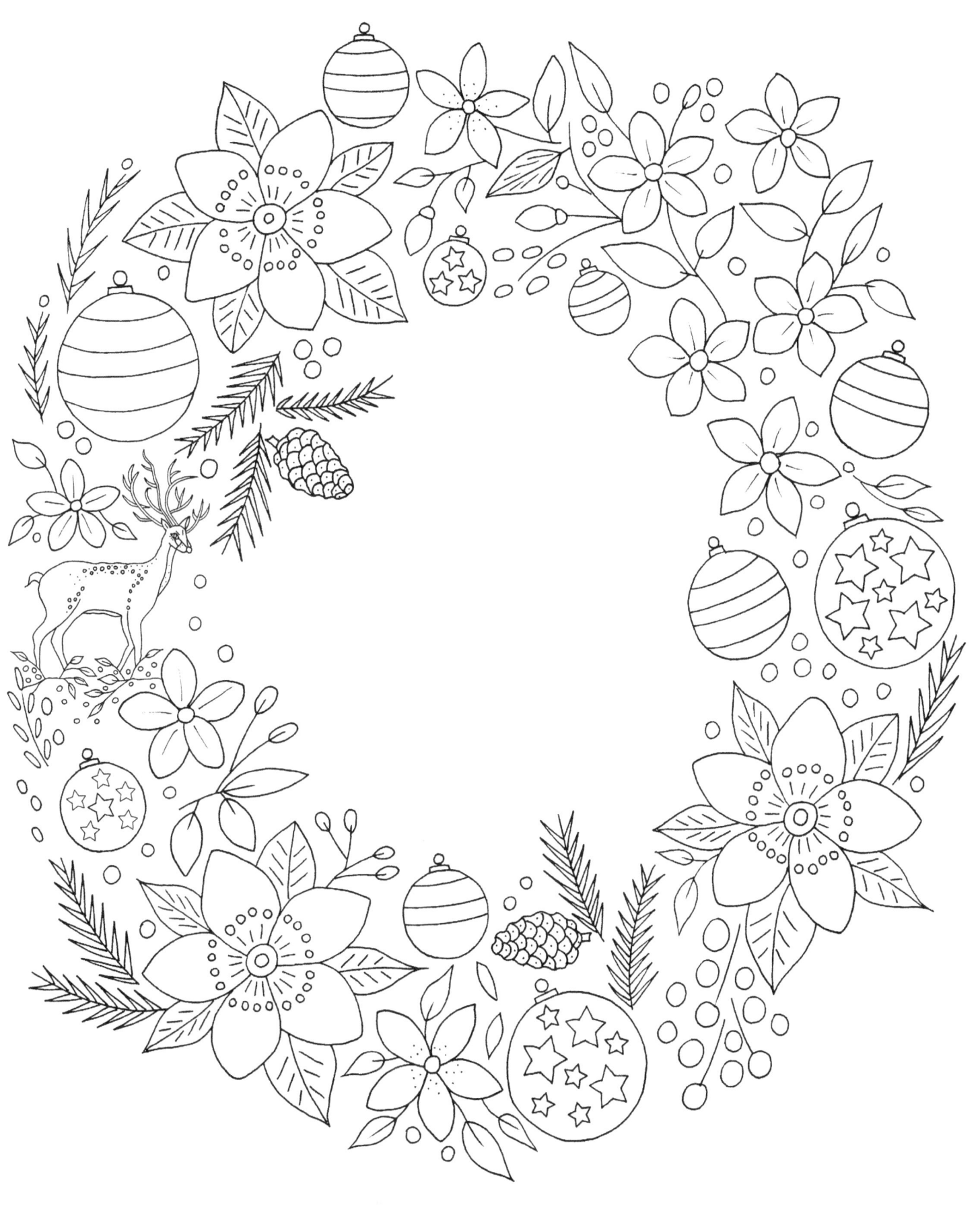

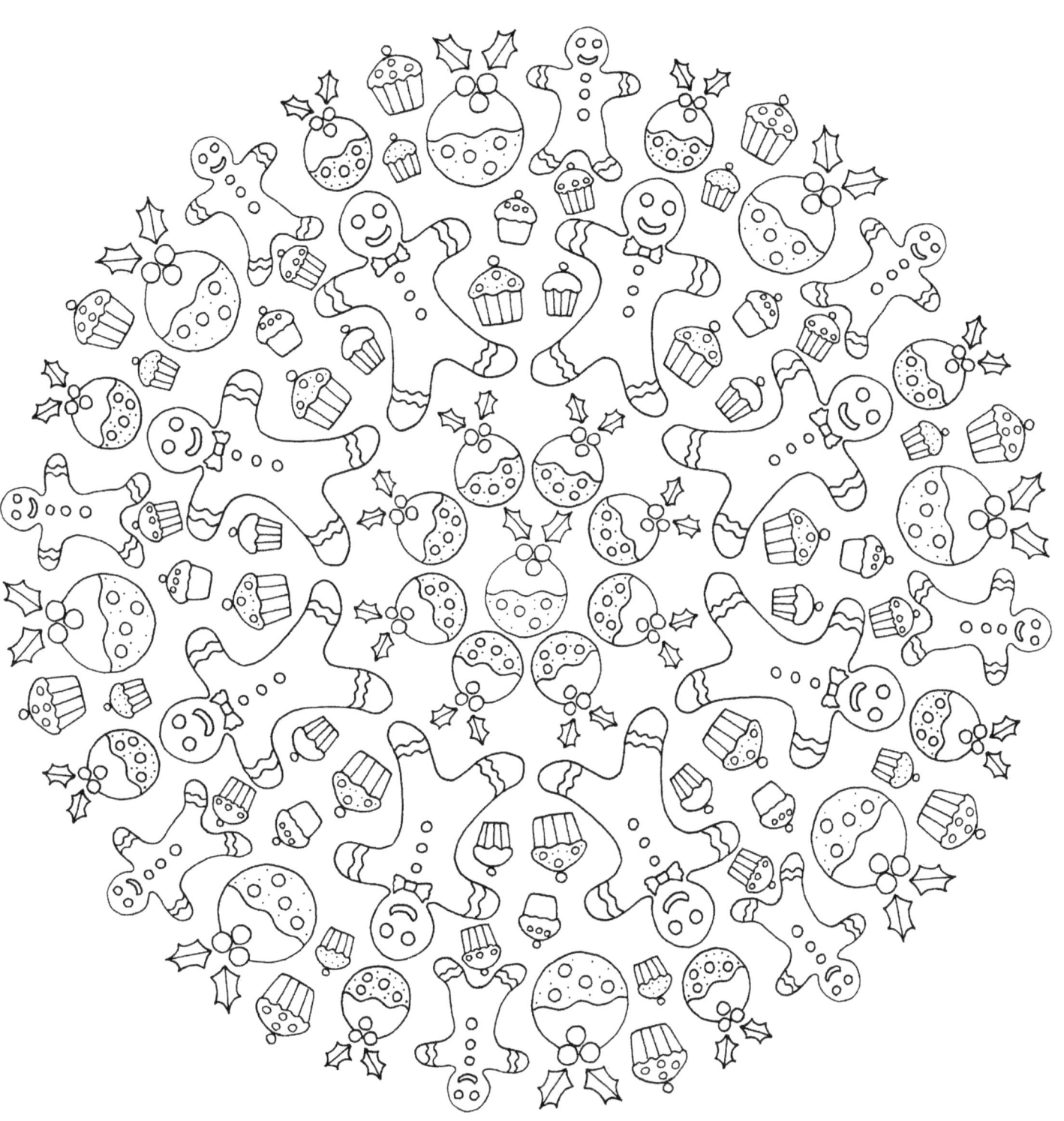

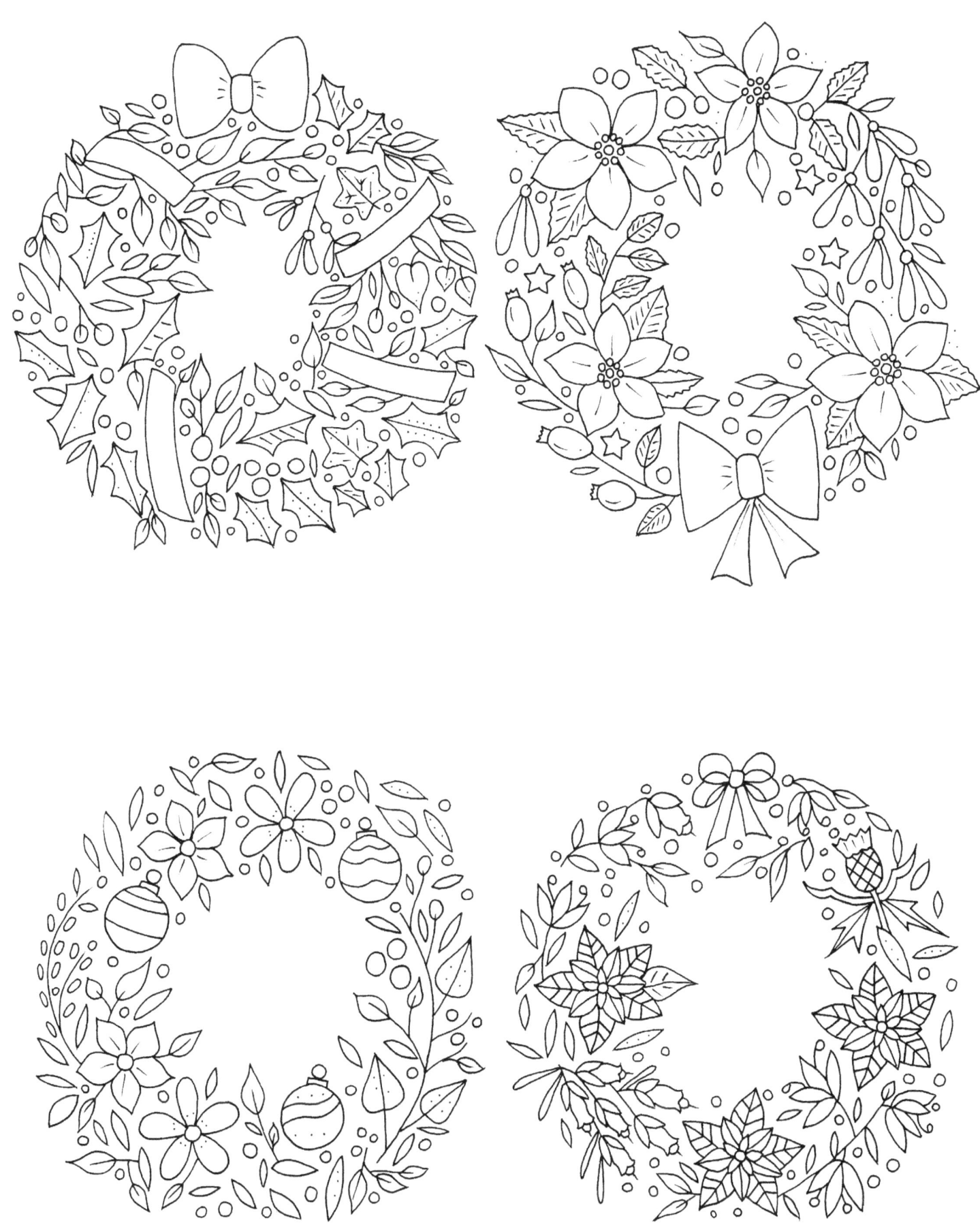

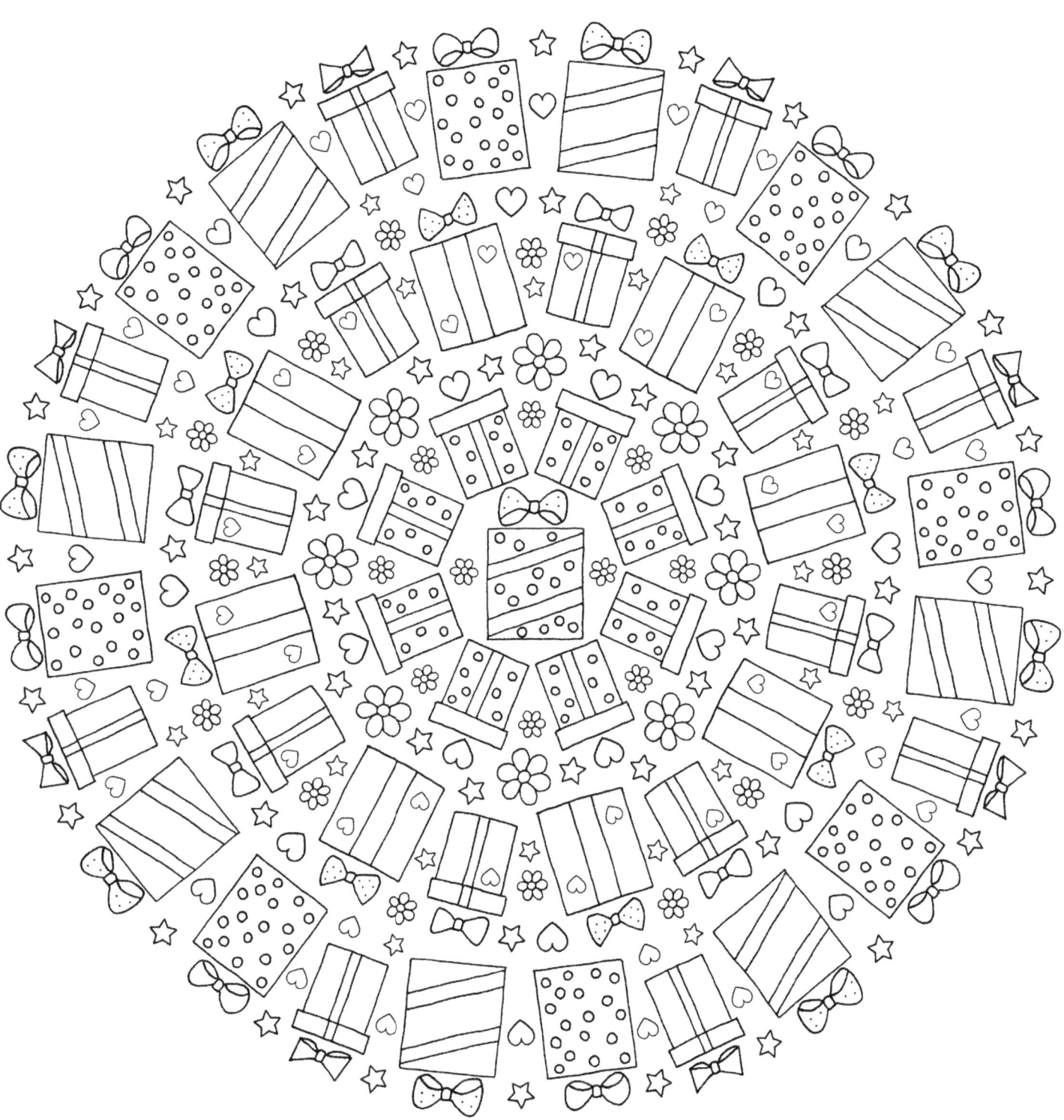

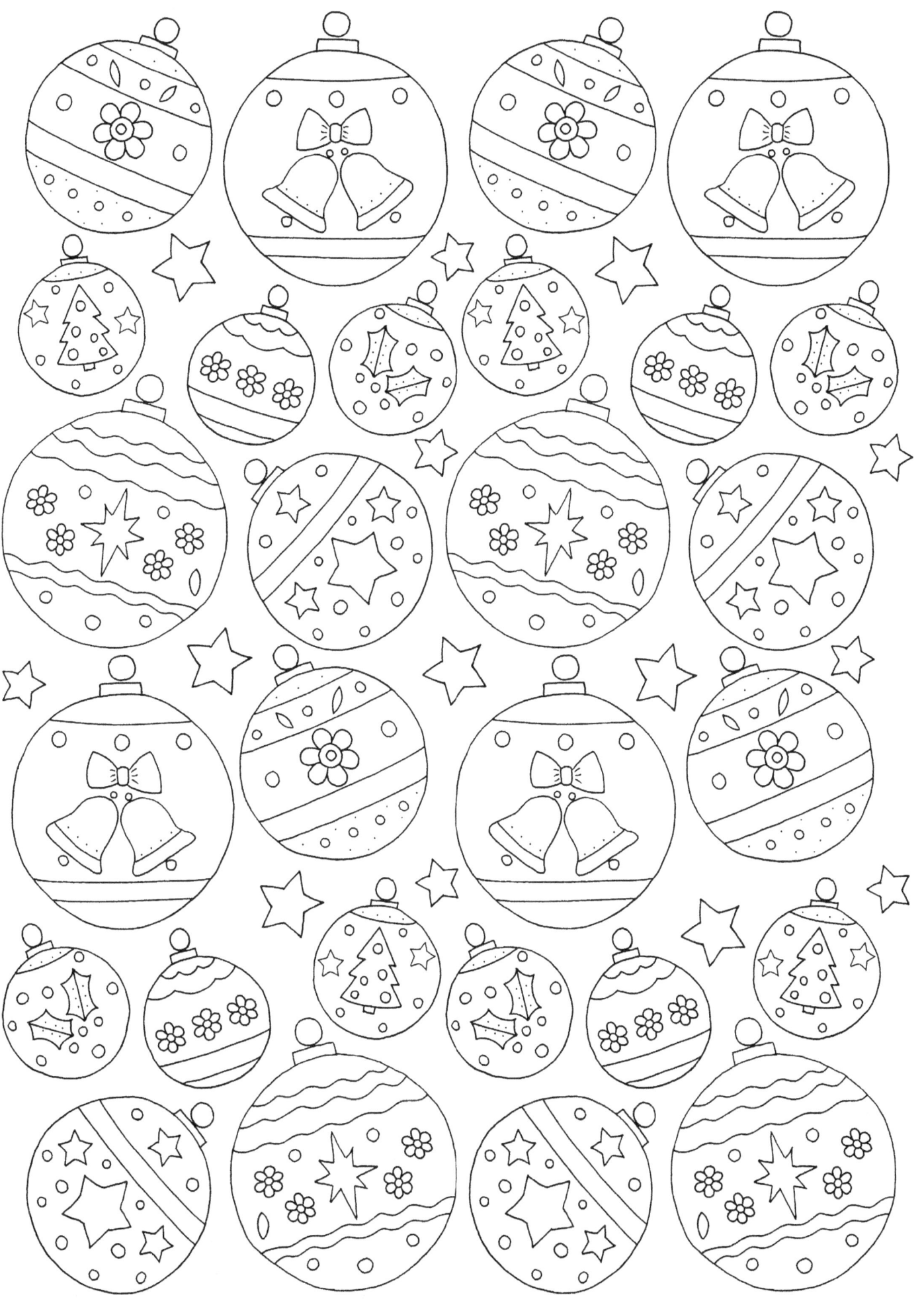

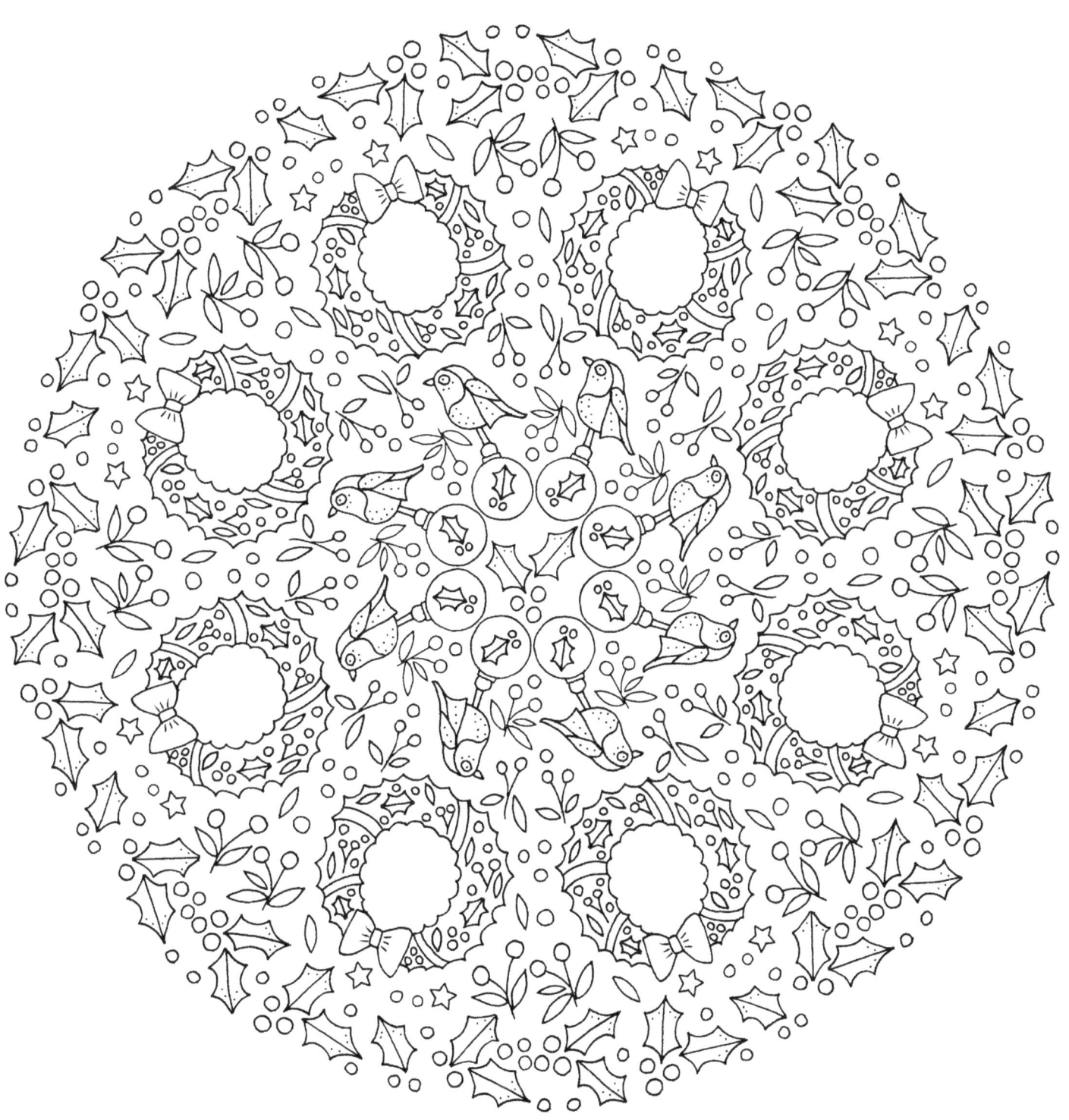

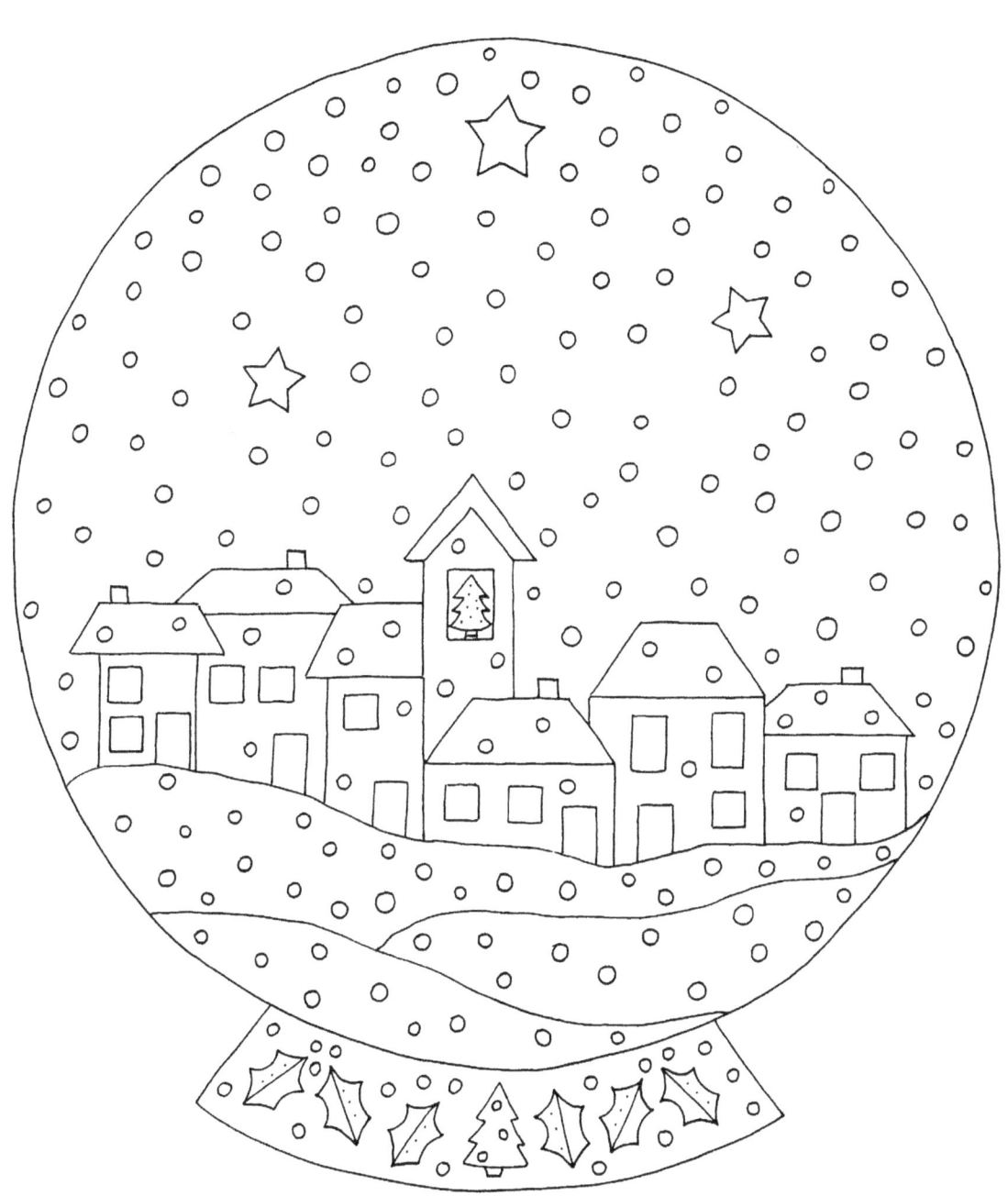

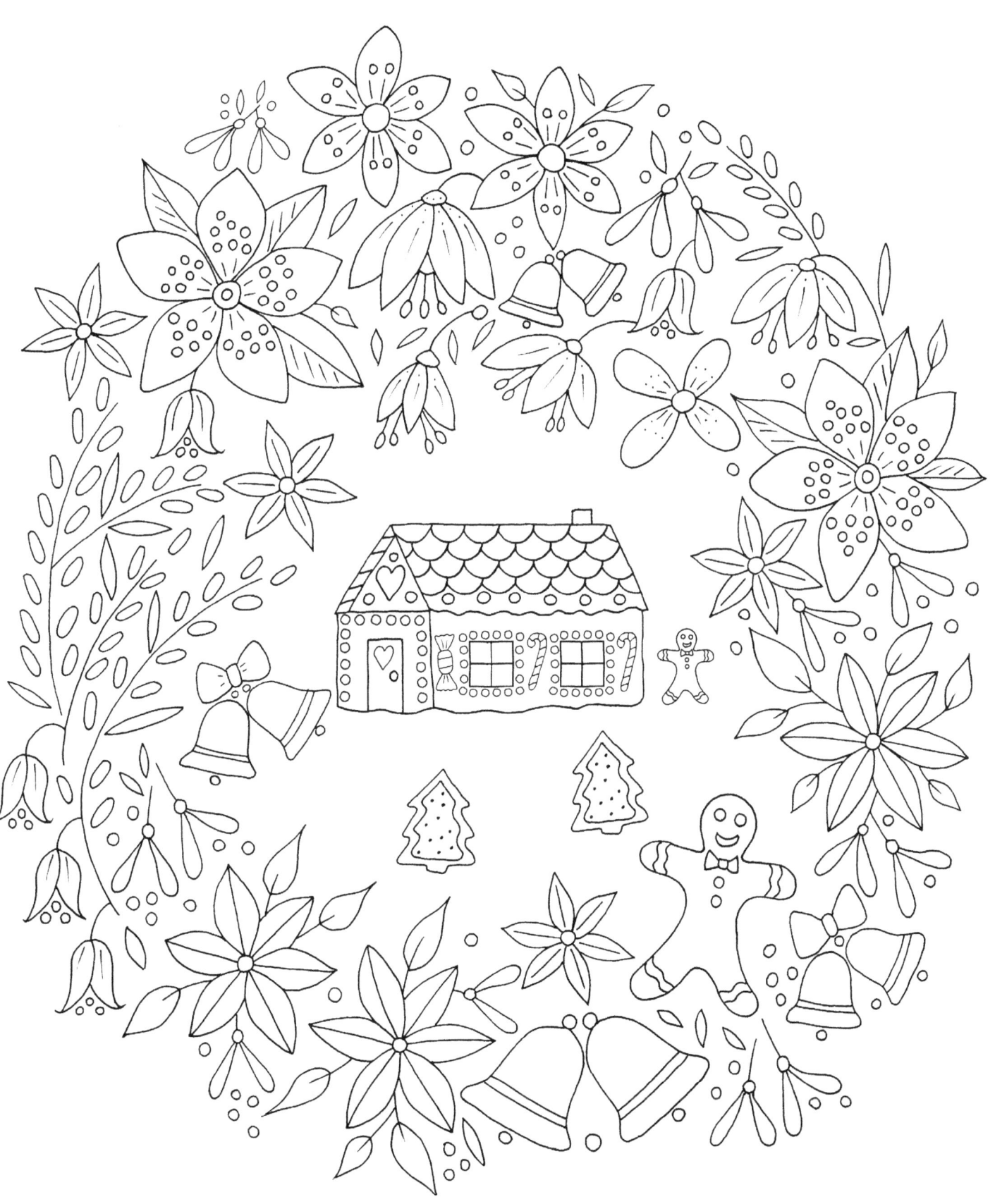

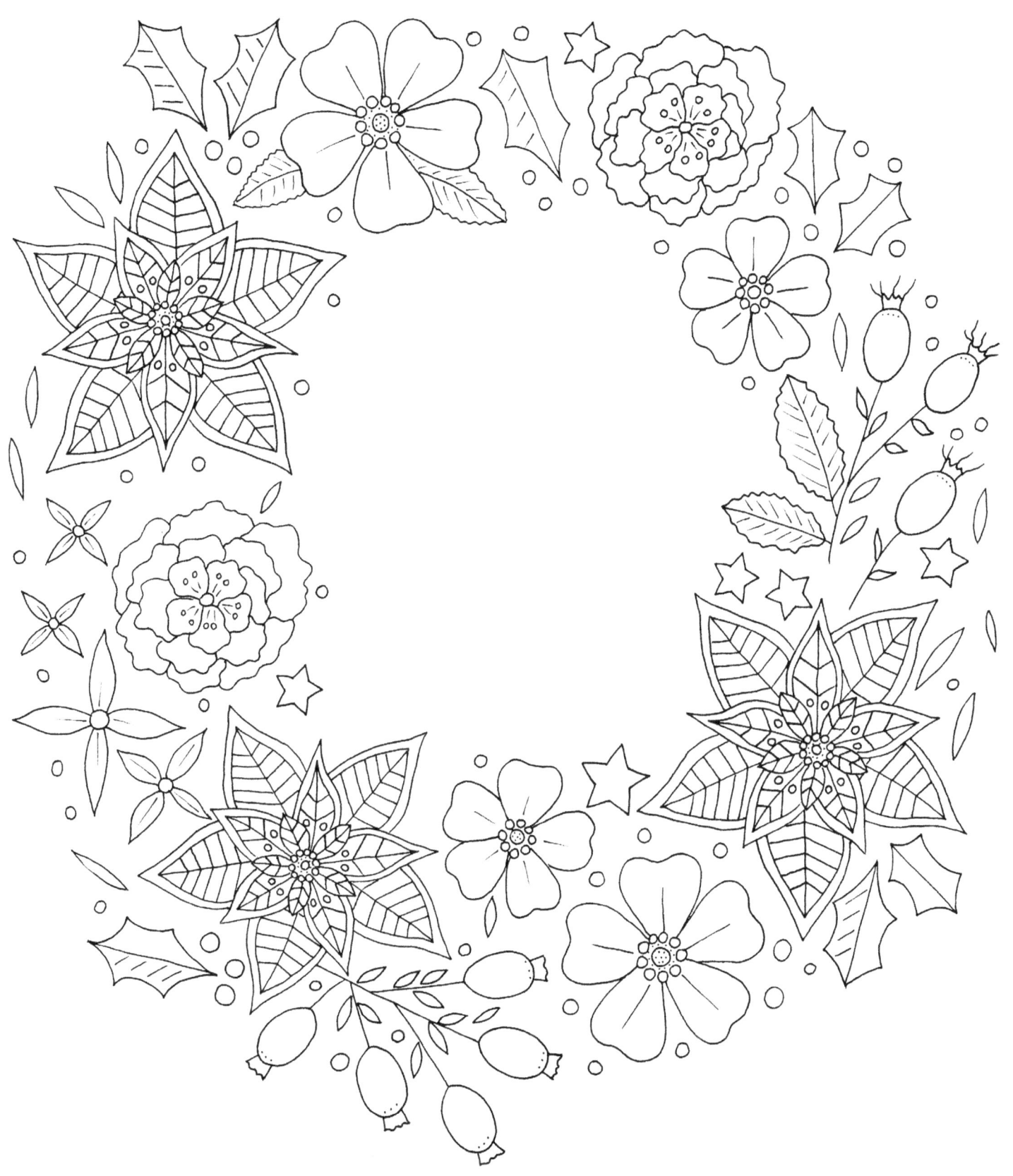

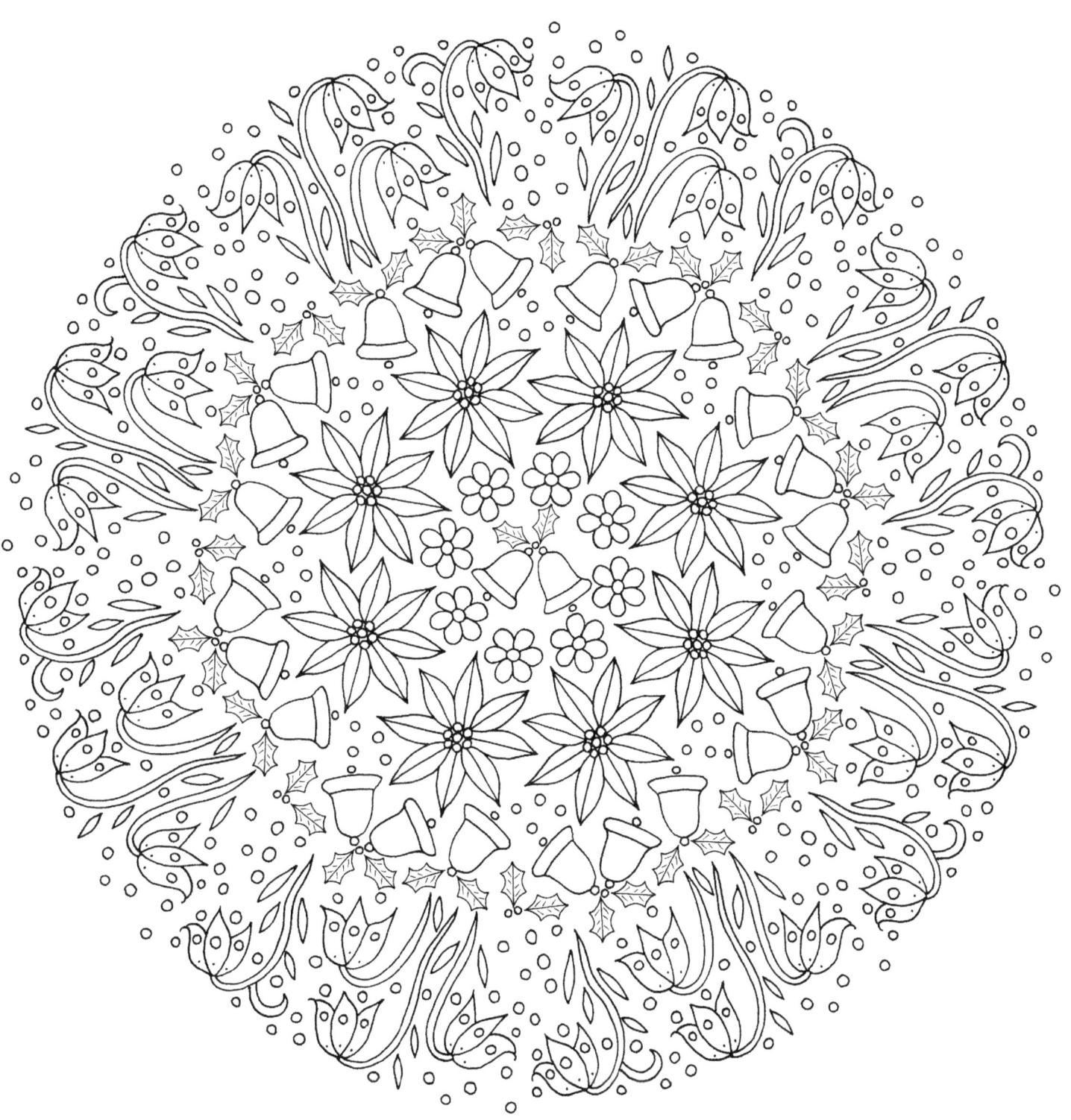

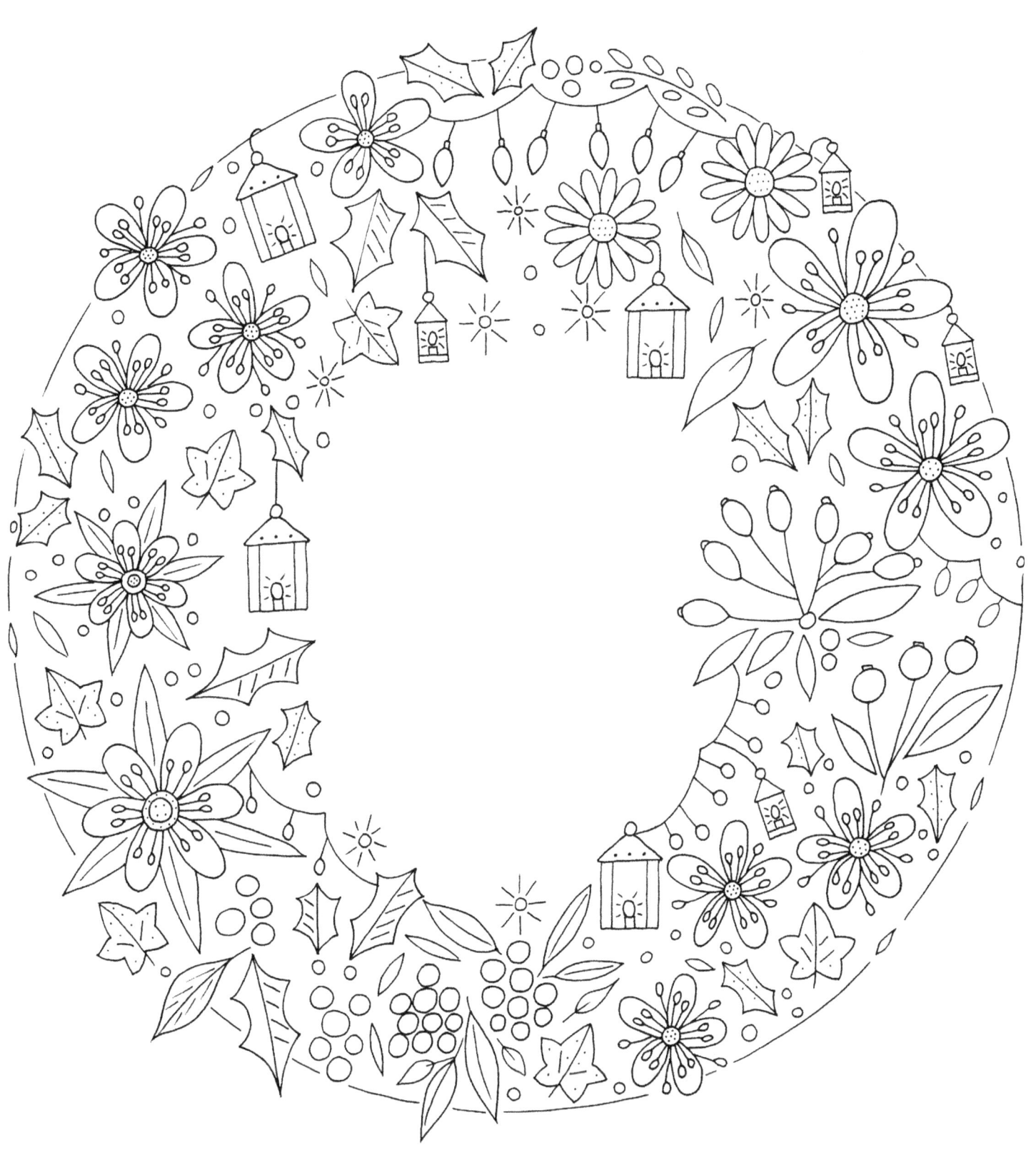

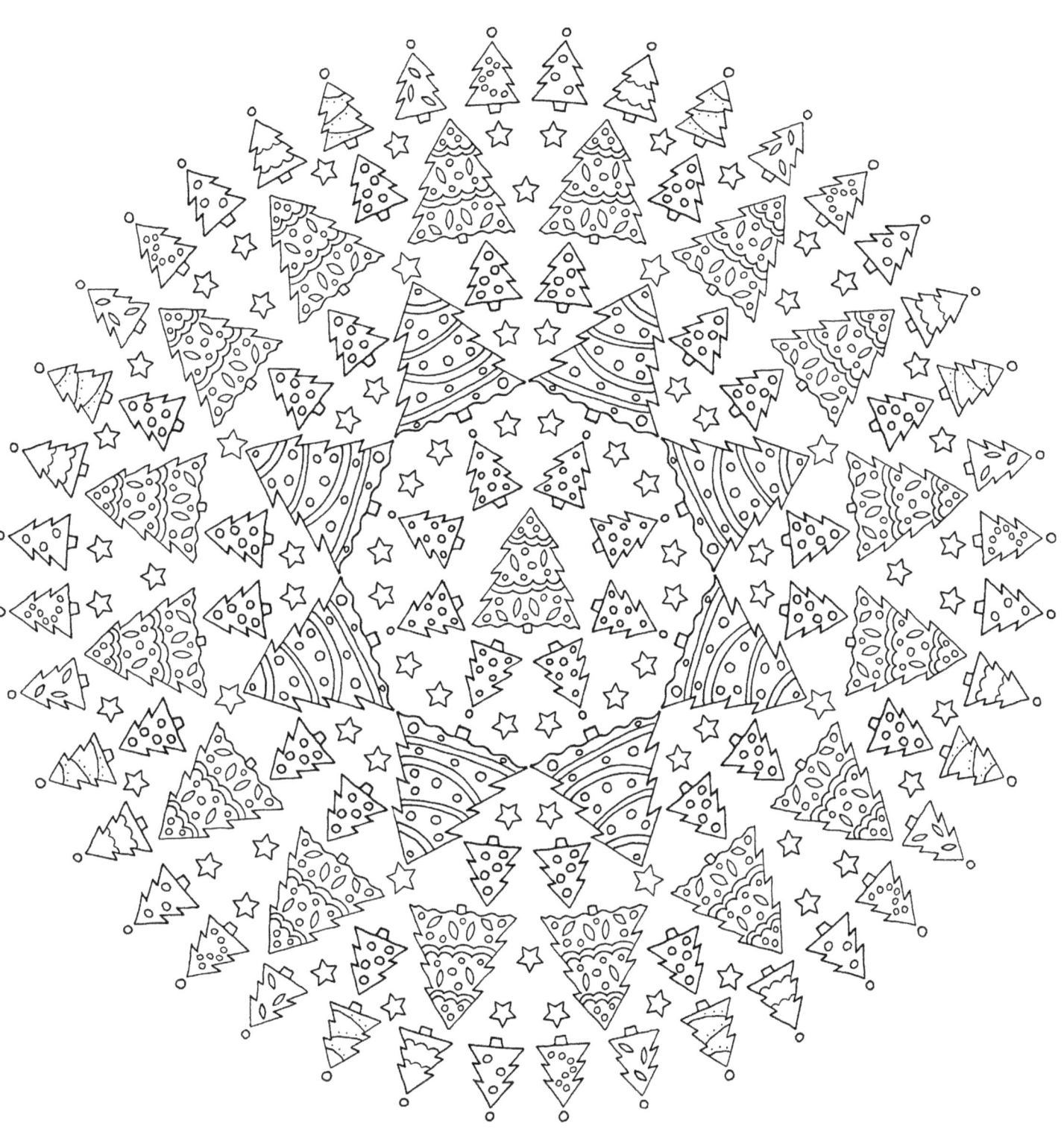

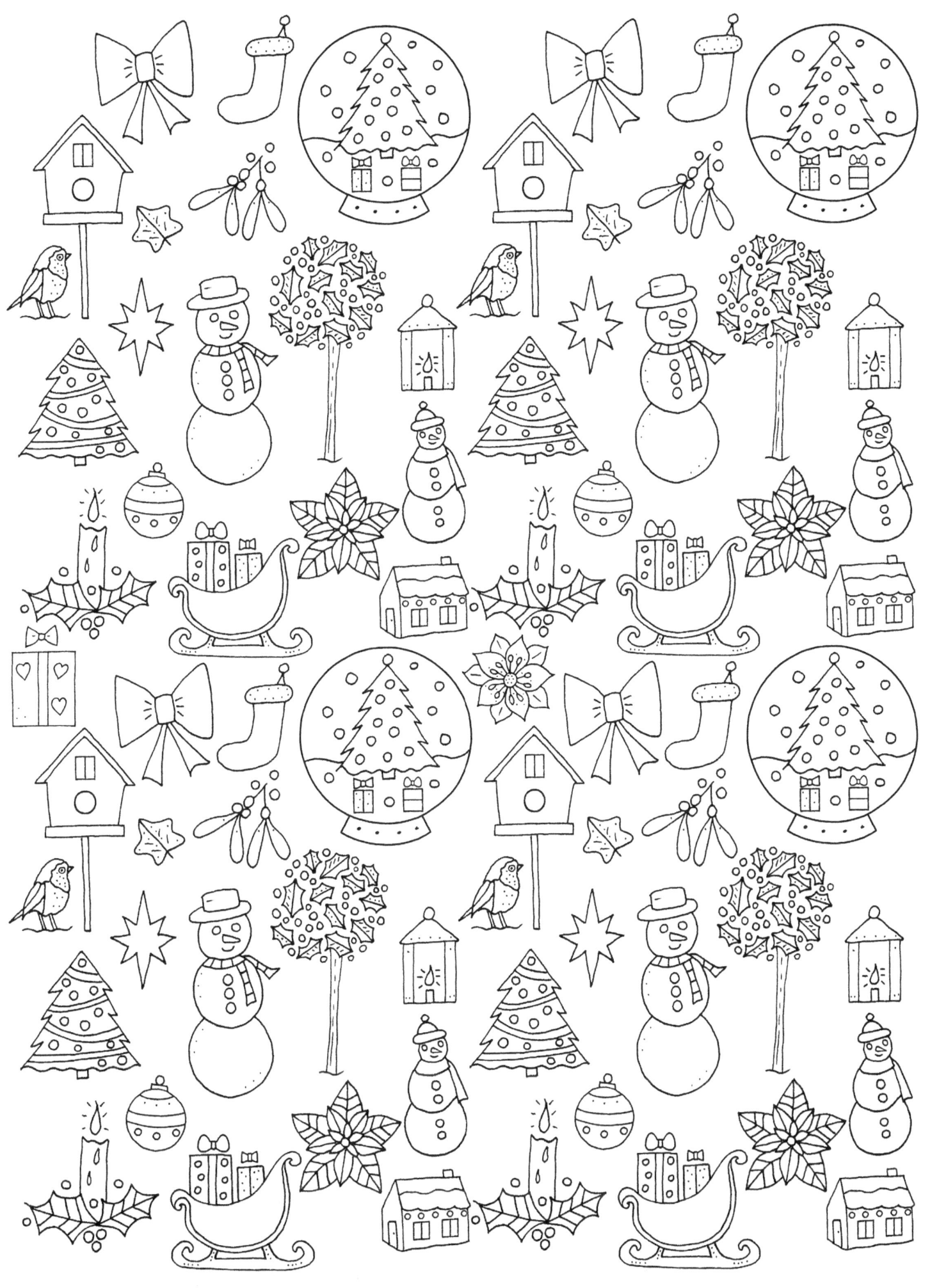

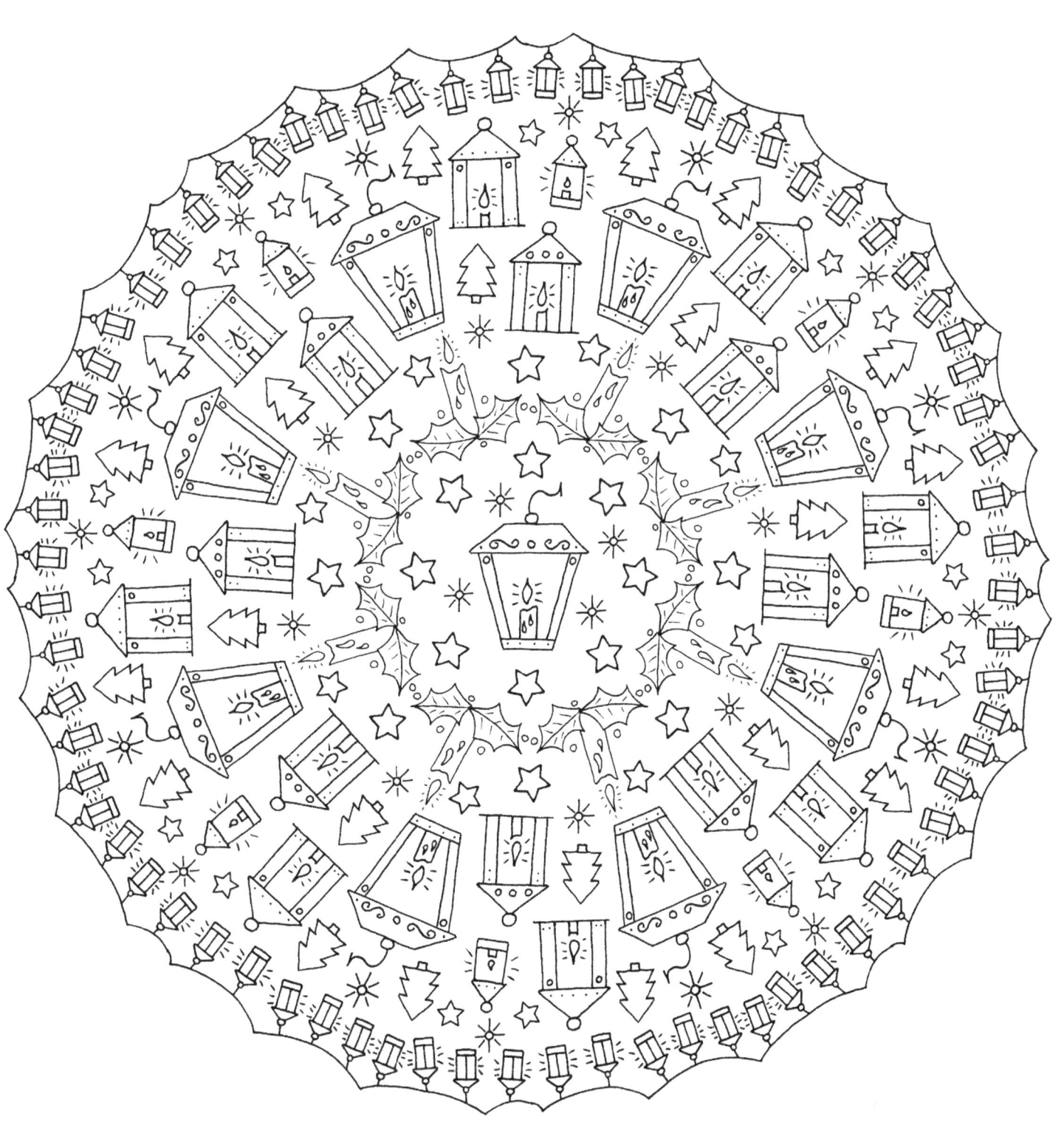

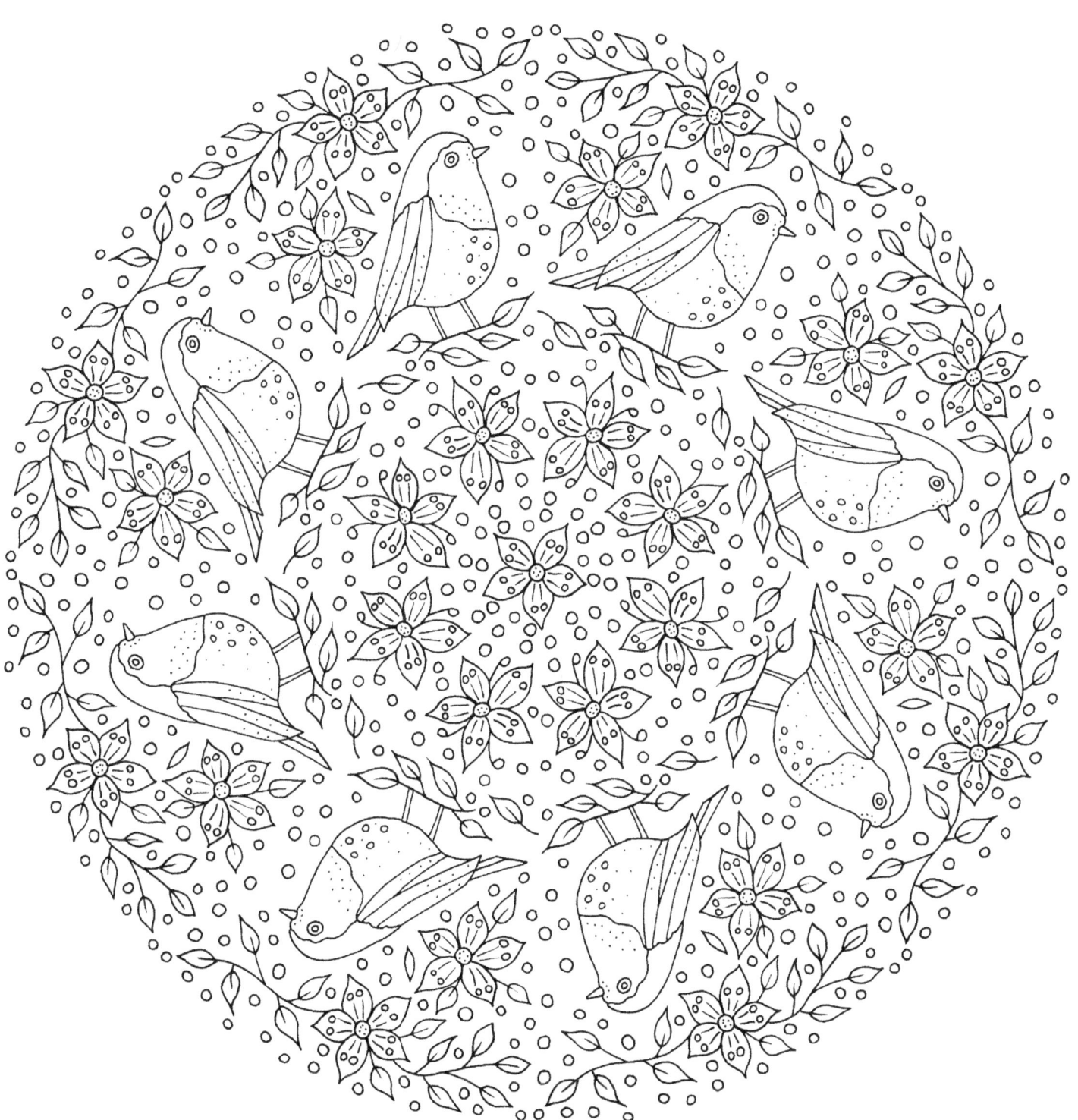

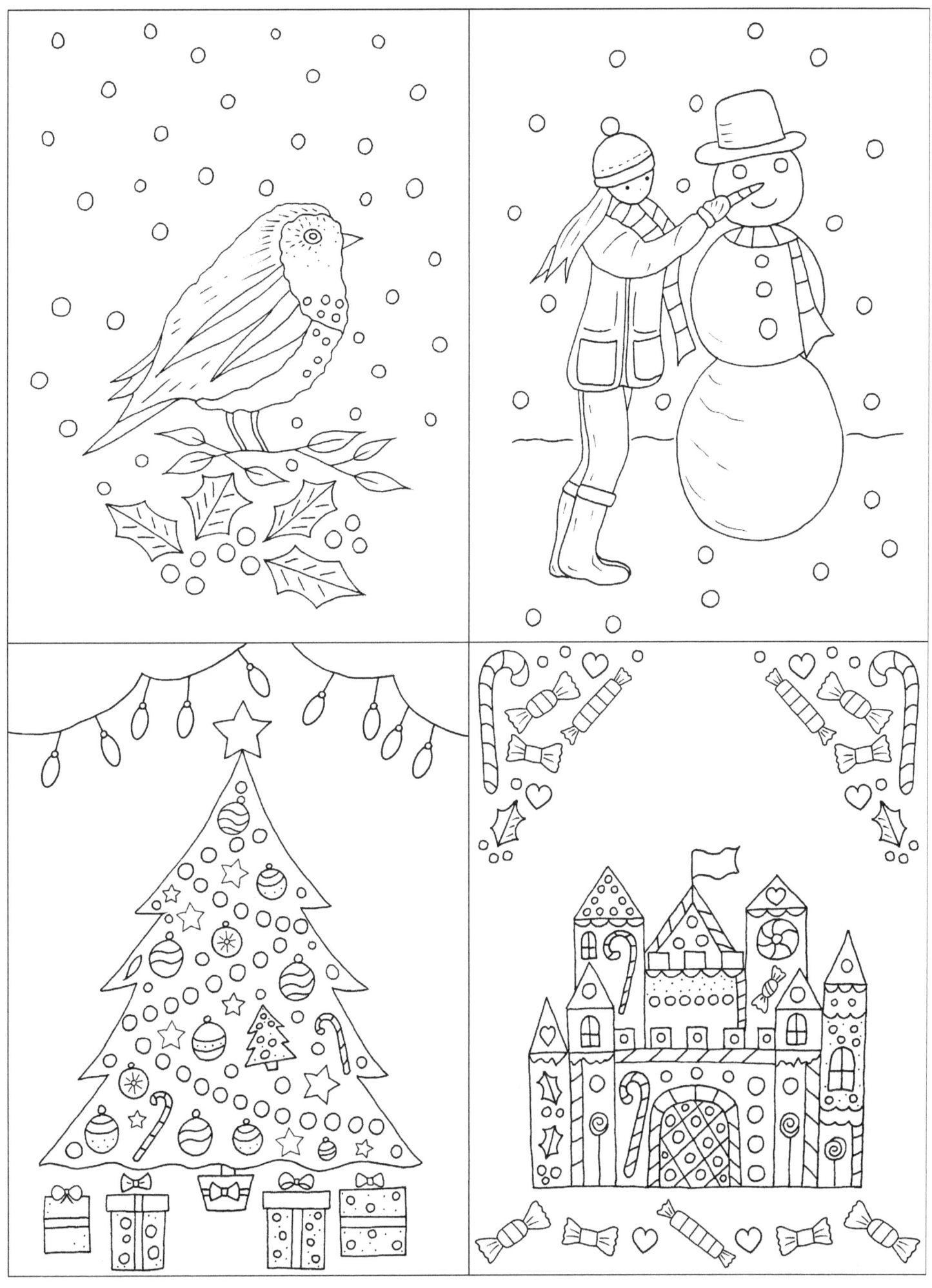